STOP BELIEVING THE LIES OTHERS SAY ABOUT YOU!

IF THIS IS LIFE

I0157594

I'M NOT GETTING OUT OF BED

STOP BELIEVING THE LIES OTHERS SAY ABOUT YOU!

IF THIS IS LIFE

I'M NOT GETTING OUT OF BED

DEBORAH ELUM

Printed in the United States of America

ISBN: 978-1-7339510-2-9
Library of Congress Control Number: 2020917414

For information, contact:

all that productions

P.O. Box 1594
Humble, Texas 77347-1594
www.allthatfilms.com

ACKNOWLEDGMENT

I give thanks to God, our Lord Jesus Christ for His love, and the Holy Spirit for His direction and wisdom.

To Randy, my husband, and my son, Brian, who I love. They both are a blessing and inspiration to me.

To my funny, witty, and beautiful mama, Lucy Peterson. To my pastor and his wife, Roy and Judy Chapman of Worship Tabernacle in Humble, Texas.

DEDICATION

I would like to dedicate this book to my friend, Birdie Mosley. Birdie is a gifted author and the inspiration behind this book project.

TODAY, I'M GOING TO STAY IN BED

Today,

I'm going to stay in bed

And pull the cover

CLEAN over my head.

If your life is

Anything like mine

Then, you know that there is never

Any peace or any quiet time.

I tried to slow down life

But it came anyway

With a cat, husband, and child

And without full time pay.

If this is LIFE
I get it, I understand
But please someone, anyone,
Please lend me a helping hand!

When I was younger, I wanted it all.
Now, if I could just have
FIVE minutes in the bathroom
Without any knocks, texts, or calls.

I made my decision
And I am putting up a sign
Please do not come in here,
I'm resting my body and my mind.

by
Deborah Elum

CONTENTS

LIES

Lies are words that are spoken or written intentionally or unintentionally that are not true to deceive or convince you that they are true.

INTRODUCTION
LIES CAN HURT YOU

I was fine under the warmth and comfort of my blanket. It was not until I got out of bed each morning that problems would come my way. Honestly, some days I didn't want to deal with anybody but me. Some days, that was enough. After I had been run over by one lie after another, I didn't feel like doing anything but hiding under the cover.

When I was four years old, I remember my sister and I sitting in the middle of a busy street playing several games of jacks. The game where we threw the ball into the air and pick up the jacks before it bounced. Once the ball bounced, we continued picking up the metal jacks.

I didn't have any fear or even think a car would dare hit us. Refusing to move, cars darted out of the way to avoid running us over. Eventually, a man walked up to us, and angrily yelled out, "You girls get out of the street before you get hit!"

I was more scared of that man yelling at me than the cars that could have wounded or even killed me. He knew that if we stayed where we were, someone would come along and run over us; either because the driver didn't see us or because they didn't care. Often, we fear the thing that saves us and put ourselves in the path of what is out to take our lives.

That is the way lies are. Lies come straight at you and will run you over. They never honked or said, "Girl, get out of the street!" Lies hurt. I mean, they can make you never want to step beyond your bedroom door. Lies come in your life to disappoint you and cause you to walk around in fear. They come to frustrate and betray you. Right in front of everybody, they will rob you of your dreams and purpose if you let them. It's almost unthinkable how words can make you throw your hands up and hand over your future.

At times, for me, and probably for you, just thinking about being held back by words is overwhelming. How can we stop believing the lies that others say about us? Girl, let me tell you how I finally came to my senses. I figured out how not to be afraid to get out of bed each morning and deal with lies and the people who tell them.

CHAPTER ONE
YOU CAN'T SAVE THE WHOLE WORLD

Over and over again, I found myself in a cycle of rescuing other people from "Life." Helping a relative, friend, or stranger get their life stabilized. It's like I had drawn them to me like a magnet. For most of my adult life, I was rescuing others, in one fashion or another.

Without me being aware of it, I was slowly being pulled into the life of other people; their conflicts, their struggles, their fights, and their troubles.

As soon as I could catch my breath, the same story started playing out again but with a different person. One by one, the next wounded soul seemed to show up on my doorstep. I found myself looking for their solution, trying to find them a home, being there to comfort them in their time of sorrow, or even helping them financially. After spending years of rescuing others, one day, I realized that I was worn out. During that time in my life, when I did get in the bed, I was zapped. I guess I should say, my body and my mind was zapped. Even when I tried to rest, my mind was thinking about them. My mind was flooded with "What if's." What if they get put out, where will they live? What if their lights get turned off, or what if they don't have money, how will they buy food?

When I would share with my Mama about the next person in my world that needed my help, she would say, "Deborah, you can't save the whole world." She was right.

I know in life, we have assignments. I really believe that. I just don't want any more wrong ones. There is nothing wrong with helping people. We are supposed to help people. The problem is when we help the wrong people.

Baby girl, you know the ones. The ones that, after everything is said and done, turn on you. They don't remember how you spent time helping, advising, or supporting them. I mean, they are quick to forget what you did for them once they are out of their situation.

You know the ones. They lead you to believe that if you don't fix it, they won't make it.

I had a relative that I helped over and over again. Not only did I support her financially, but also I gave her some good advice along with it. After I woke up to the truth about her, I realized that she never took any of my advice. Most people in trouble want your time, your money, and your ear. But as for your advice, there will be very few that will put it into use. So, unless they ask, I learned to keep my mouth shut and to be quick to hear and slow to speak.

Girl, I knew that I had to pull the financial plug. Sometimes you have to and it's just like that. It's not easy, but it's necessary. Giving my relative money was not the answer anymore. In fact, it was enabling her not to do any better for herself. She started to be dependent upon me to fix her problem every time. A person that can't do better is different than a person who refuses to do better. You really need to be able to distinguish between the two.

You know what I found out? She survived! I was not her only ace in the hole. She kept living and doing exactly what she always did; spending all her own money on drinking, gambling, and smoking.

It is not our job to rescue every soul that gets wounded. There were times when we may have tried to. I don't know why we think we need to. We may want to and even think we have to, but we have to realize that we can't save the whole world as women. The world was in a mess long before we got here and when we leave, it will still be in a mess.

Our part is to only clean up other people's messes that we are supposed to. We need to discover where our part begins and ends. We can't play the role of the Savior. If we do, we will get to the point where He will show us that we are not and never will be.

You can't help someone who only wants you to fix it for them all the time. They don't want to solve the problem themselves. That is the bottom line. One thing about people, when they think their situation is hopeless, they always want you to jump in the troubled waters and swim out to save them. They expect you to rescue their families, jobs, home, business, relationships, or organization. Not in all cases but in many, they had plenty of opportunities to get out of the situation long before the currents of desperation pushed them out into the deep waters. They just would not get out of the water until they were sinking.

There I go once again, finding myself out of the boat and swimming over to them. It was hard, but I had to stop believing the lie that everybody that came my way needed me to rescue them. I am learning to stay out of the water and throw them out a life preserver.

You also need to stay out of the water. It might be advice or only support, but whatever you need to do, don't let people cling on to you so tight for dear life that they take you under. In life, there will always be people that refuse to grab for truth. Always.

CHAPTER TWO
STAYING FOCUSED

I had allowed myself to get to the place of being known as "Ms. Fix It." As requests kept coming in for help, I volunteered or allowed myself to be volunteered. I didn't realize how I was focused on wanting to please people. My slogan must have been, "Call me, I will do it for you."

I believed that lie until I had lost me. The "me" that was bold, outgoing, outspoken, and confident.

The one that enjoyed writing, having a cup of tea, reading my Bible more, and taking time talking with friends. So many people were in my life not because they really enjoyed me but because I was always doing something for them. I was always on the go!

In high school, I excelled and soared like an eagle. It seemed only yesterday when I was in high school sitting in my English class. The years seemed to have shifted me from just a child to womanhood without any stops along the way.

By the time I finished college, this eagle wanted to hide in a cave and puck out all her feathers. I was married, had a son, career, and overwhelmed with church responsibilities. I struggled to find that soaring eagle again.

You have to protect you. You have to take control of your life and set boundaries to protect yourself. Yes, protect yourself from being manipulated, used, overworked, or violated by others and yourself. I am learning from experience that staying balanced means staying focused. You will find out sooner or later that you are not SUPERWOMAN.

Who am I? I mean, really? I started having conversations with myself. You need to ask yourself the same questions. As women, we all need some downtime all by ourselves. We are not women who just take care of other folks' business ALL THE TIME. We are real people with real feelings, desires, purpose, and destiny.

Too many of us, at one time or another, didn't realize how talented, creative, and innovative we are. Not just in one area of our lives but in all of them if we would recognize it. If we don't slow down, we will never find out the truth. It's time to slow down and not let lies continue to feed on our time, energy, finances, and ability to succeed in life. In other words, it is time to stop feeding the lies!

My Mama would put it like this, "If you stop feeding every stray dog that comes around, they will stop hanging around." The same is true with lies that come into your head. Stop feeding them. Stop accepting them and stop entertaining them. If you do, guess what? They will stop coming for a meal when you start believing and speaking the truth about who you are.

CHAPTER THREE

YOU DON'T NEED TO FIGURE IT ALL OUT

One thing about life is that you can't expect to figure it all out overnight. Life is an ongoing, problem solving, day-by-day process. Each day has its own challenges, worries, joys, strengths, and victories.

Like the day I was outside picking plums from my tree. One moment I was enjoying the day, and the next, I was in excursing pain. I couldn't stand up. I slowly made my way into the house and got into the bed.

Later that night, I was in so much pain that my husband rushed me to an emergency room. The doctor on call gave me a few prescriptions, but none of them helped. After a few days, I went to see my primary physician. I thought that surely he had the answer.

When I left his office, the impression I got from my visit was like he didn't even believe me or that I was making the whole thing up. He did write me some new prescriptions to take, but the pain was still exactly the same as before.

Weeks after my injury, I was using a desk chair to get around the house to cook and clean up what I could. Finally, after many calls to my doctor's office, I got a prescription from him for a wheelchair.

The next stop was a chiropractor's office. After his examination, he offered no hope but was willing to start treatment. After a month, I could tell that it helped but not nearly enough.

I was led to contact a doctor in a different network. Within less than one week, the two prescriptions she prescribed for me were working. Before the wheelchair arrived, I canceled the order myself because I knew I had found the answer. After two months of treatment, she released me, and I could walk upright without any pain or any medication.

Don't get me wrong because, during that six-month journey, my body was screaming lies at me all day and most of the night. Lies tried to convince me that I would never walk again and that I would always be in pain.

A lie always wants you to think there is no hope. That is a BIG LIE. For you, it might not be a back injury. It may be a broken heart or a broken relationship. Not everyone will be compassionate as you suffer through the pain. Not everyone will even understand or give you any hope that you will ever be okay again.

Someone has the answer you need. Maybe not at this very moment and perhaps not even tomorrow, but the answer will come as you keep seeking after it. There is an answer somewhere out there. I realized that just because a person knew how to help me yesterday does not mean that they have an answer today.

That is why we should not be afraid of change. Change is a good solution when it brings about the answer that makes us better, stronger, and whole.

Some solutions don't come overnight. Solutions come in many different shapes, sizes, and colors. Just don't accept that there is not one for you.

CHAPTER FOUR
BE YOUR OWN CHEERLEADER

You have to have a reason for getting up every morning. You have to be a part of something that makes a difference. It is that which gives you the drive and motivation to go beyond your bedroom door. You have to be your own cheerleader and encourage yourself. Pull out your pom poms and cheer for your own successes.

I always wanted to write a book, but I could not find the time to get it done. I gathered many excuses for myself. I had a whole pile of them. The first one on the pile was that I just did not have the time. There were many excuses.

What if I don't get the money to publish it and how will I market the book? The excuses seemed more than a mile high.

When I was meeting with my friend, Mary Barnes, I glanced over at a book on her coffee table and noticed her name on the front cover.

Mary was one of the busiest people I had ever met. I questioned her about how she found the time to write. She owned and ran three successful beauty salon chains. She was the producer and host of her own radio talk show, "Let's Talk Heart-to-Heart." She was the treasurer of her neighborhood civic club and was the assistant coordinator of her church's senior group. She put on fundraisers to help those who experienced financial hardships, just to name some of the things she did. That is when I thought to myself, if Mary did it, I can do it too. That is when all the excuses stopped.

Sometimes, I could only write during my lunch hour at work or five minutes before I went to work. It took years to finish, but I did. You can't let time determine if you will do it or not. It might only take you a week. It might take months or it might take years to achieve something that is within you. The only thing that matters is, did you finish it?

I was so excited that I did it. I sent the manuscript to a large publishing house that accepted it. I thought I had found a solution only to find out later that they wanted to change one of the characters from being just a busy body to being seductive, get a man any way you can, woman. The book went from being G-rated to R-rated. When I disagreed with the character changes, they did not want to publish it and sent the manuscript back to me with a rejection letter. That rejection was the fuel I needed to move to the next phase.

I was working by then and I saved the money to get it published. The day I got the copies in the mail, I celebrated. I was holding in my hand what was once only a vision. When I sold the first copy, I was on cloud nine. All the time, commitment, and investment had paid off. It felt wonderful.

What if you don't have a cheerleader in your corner? You have to be able to keep believing in yourself even when no one believes in you, but you. Finding someone that believes in your dream is not easy. There will always be the ones that don't want you to succeed, ones that tell you that you can't do it, or give you excuses why you can't do it. You have to be your own cheerleader. Yell, scream, and cheer the loudest for you.

My childhood was my cheerleader's training camp. When I was in high school, I was on the track team. Of all the races I ran, my family never attended a race. Not one. I was determined to go to track meets and cheer for myself. I was always my best fan and my head cheerleader. I learned I had to be.

When I won the award for the most outstanding student of my Spanish Club, no family was there to cheer me on. There were many other times that I didn't get support for what I achieved. So don't let that be a reason you don't do it. All you need to do is to keep going. I want to encourage you to get those pom poms ready, girl, because you can do it as long as you believe in yourself!

CHAPTER FIVE

YOU CAN'T DANCE ALL THE TIME

I can still picture a scene from a movie I was watching when I was five years old. There stood a casually dressed woman who looked like she may have just gotten off work. As she stepped through a large, white door frame, she was transformed into this elegant woman in a beautiful long white flowing ball gown.

She didn't have a care in the world as she danced and spun around. Then, a man in a tuxedo appeared and stepped through the door frame. As he swooped her up in his arms, they began to dance together. I was so excited. I just knew that was how life was meant to be. I watched and thought about how I couldn't wait to grow up.

At five, I really thought that was how people lived; not a care in the world. I had no idea that when the cameras were turned off, and the lights were dimmed, that same woman had to put on her regular clothes, take off her stage makeup, and go home to a real family and her own real problems.

There were so many things going on between the ages of four through the age of thirteen. Everything about my life was always drastically changing. By the time I was thirteen, my oldest brother had moved away from home, followed by my oldest sister, who married her high school sweetheart and moved out. The biggest change of all was when my mother got married again. My life became sandwiched between high school and more family members.

Our new family was now four stepbrothers, one stepsister, three younger sisters, three younger brothers, stepfather, mother, and a dog. It was abnormal normalcy every day. Since my parents could not find a house large enough for all of us that they could afford, they came up with a workable plan. Both of our homes were across the street from each other and we would live in both of them.

We ate meals and watched television together until it was time to go to bed. At night, the boys slept in one house and all the girls and my parents slept in the other one.

Our family seemed like a thousand-piece jigsaw puzzle. Although the pieces were on the table, we each tried to put it together without looking at the picture on the box. I was glad that my oldest brother and sister had gotten out just in time. Even at thirteen years old, I was ready to move out too if I could have found a man who would marry me. Thankfully, that did not happen at the time.

I didn't know what a normal family looked like at all. Not a clue. There were many days when I just couldn't dance. Not only could I not dance, but also I didn't even remember how.

I would hear lies from a family member telling me that I would never amount to anything. It was rough during those years, but I knew what they were saying was not the truth.

I started seeing school as a place that was getting me ready to dance. Except for Mrs. Phillips, my third-grade teacher, I always had a teacher who would encourage me that there was a white door frame for me. One day, I would step right through the door frame to the other side and be transformed into something beautiful.

Sister, if you want to be transformed, you have to believe in yourself and step through the white door frame of hope. That is the place that reveals the great purpose in you where you can always dance.

CHAPTER SIX

DON'T BE SHOCKED

"It takes two to argue and one person arguing by themselves looks like a fool." Mama always said to me when my sister, Joyce, and I would get into a disagreement. I never wanted to be the fool, so I would let her argue by herself. Those words would follow me throughout my life. That's why I refuse to argue even with a lie.

As I walked into a crowded room of associates, different groups of people were standing around talking. Many were discussing how informative the meeting had been or what they were planning to have for lunch.

I spotted a friend of mine as she stood face to face with another woman. So I headed over to join in their conversation. I could hear one of them talking and I could tell she was really fired up about something. When I got closer, I was ready to join in the conversation, but they were not talking about the meeting at all. The topic was "Deborah Elum." I admit that I was surprised. No, shocked by what was being said.

When my friend, Lane, looked up, I could see her eyes looking straight at me as I stood behind the other woman. She tried to signal her to shut up but it took her a minute to get the hint. I just stood there like a statue as their conversation had me speechless. Not once did I hear my friend defend me or tell her that she was wrong about what she said about me.

That night, I laid in bed with the cover up to my neck as tears rolled down my face. I had plenty of time to think about what had taken place earlier that day. I knew it was all lies. I mean, lies with a capital "L."

But, why couldn't I stand up for myself and set her straight? Why didn't I defend myself, my character, and my reputation? What were the other people thinking about me who had overheard them?

I was humiliated. I mean down to the core. Neither the other woman nor my friend apologized. I never could bring myself to address it with either one of them, which made me feel worse. I had done nothing wrong.

I was not the woman she described, nor did I do the things she said I did. Yet, I was hurt by the lies that had been spoken. I became that little girl in first grade all over again, the girl who was ignored by the other little girls.

I had been in the hospital for a medical condition for a year. When I was released, the school year had already started. So when I began attending first grade, the other girls viewed me as an outsider. Those little girls already had boyfriends. I even overheard one of them saying that I was trying to steal their boyfriends. I could not believe that they felt threatened by me, a shy little girl who enjoyed playing with snails, climbing trees, and had no interest in having a boyfriend at that age.

I could handle my own at home, but once I walked through the front door at school, I changed into the "She's just shy" little girl. That is what my uncles called me, and I believed it.

Lies don't fight fair. They will hit you with every bit of meanness they have. People can use them in very cruel ways. Lies can be bitter, jealous, unfair, humiliating, and insulting. Lies try to convince you that you are not good enough, not pretty enough, not strong enough, or smart enough.

Lies come at you all the time. When it comes to lies, you will never be good enough. They are spoken to make sure you will never measure up. You have to realize that you are good enough, smart enough, courageous enough, and pretty enough.

I had given years to so many unfruitful things from relationships, jobs, and organizations that just tolerated me and really didn't appreciate me.

Dr. Mike Murdock said something that really helped me. He said, "Go where you are celebrated instead of where you are tolerated." That standard has helped me determine the right people who need to be in my life, whether from a job, church, or friends. So I go where people appreciate, celebrate, and value me.

When I was in third grade, my sister, Joyce, and I would stop by a field on the way home. It was full of grass that was known as sour grass. We would pull up some of it, swallow the juice, and spit out the stems—that how life is. You have to chew, get the juice out, and spit out the part you don't need.

People are always going to talk about you, whether they say something good or something bad. Just accept that. Don't be shocked by what they say, just learn to chew and spit out the lies because you don't need to swallow any of them.

CHAPTER SEVEN
I DON'T BELIEVE THIS

"I don't believe this," I said as I shook my head. If I had only known the truth earlier. Here I was looking at a copy of my birth certificate. There it was in black and white!

Now, as I was getting ready for college, I saw it on a copy of my birth certificate. My first name was not there. Not the name I knew. From the first day of first grade until I finished high school, my name had been recorded as Debra. My aunt had even taught me to spell it that way. For twelve years of my life, I lived with a lie and didn't even know it.

Written in black ink was my real name, Deborah. I thought *no one noticed the error? No one noticed the lie?* For twelve years of my life, my name was misspelled. No one even cared?

The wrong name was all over every homework paper I turned in, on every report card, every school record, every prescription I took as a child, and even my medical records. It was everywhere. I was so disappointed that absolutely no one noticed. I think that's when the lies started that no one cared about me.

That lie of "No one cares about me" would surface in my life at different times. One time, I was throwing a BIG Pity Party and I was the only one invited. That evening, I cried what seemed like hours. The party theme was, "I prayed for everybody and no one is praying for me."

That Sunday, Joe Moles was the guest speaker at my church. After the message, he shared words of encouragement with different people. He turned to me and said, "Deborah, I have been praying for

I DON'T BELIEVE THIS

you." I had only met him one time before and this man was praying for me? From that day on, that was the last Pity Party I ever had.

I am thankful that God sends people our way to let us know how much He cares about us. We have to realize that people do care. If it's not our family, then it's a teacher that cares. If it's not a teacher, then it might be a neighbor, your hairstylist, or even a person driving right by you. So it's time to throw the cover back, jump out of that bed, put on your party hat, your high heels, and crank up the music. Throw yourself a "Thankfulness Party" for all the people who care about you!

CHAPTER EIGHT
YOU HAVE THE OTHER GLASS SLIPPER

Do you remember the story of Cinderella? She could never work hard enough to please her mean stepmother and jealous stepsisters. The end of the story is what I took note of. She refused to let a life-changing opportunity pass her by.

In the story, it was known that whoever fits the glass slipper would marry the prince. When she was freed from her room, she ran for an opportunity to try on the glass slipper. However, her stepmother tripped the king's servant, causing the glass slipper to land on the floor and shatter into pieces. What her stepmother did not know was that Cinderella had the other glass slipper in her apron pocket. Girl, she pointed her toes, put the slipper on her foot, and stepped into her future.

What does that mean? It means that you have the other glass slipper. All you have to do is put it on and step into your future too. Don't let lies, disappointment, and fear keep you locked away in your room. You were created beautiful, inside and out.

So many times, I was in bed with my head covered up in shame, humiliation, and frustration. Like the time when I became friends with a woman named Ira.

I remembered once she told me that she was my only friend. I had no idea what she meant because I had friends long before I met her. Two of my friends stopped me one day to warn me about her. "Ira is telling us all of the terrible things that you are saying about us. Not only that, but she is also telling everybody what you said about them too," they said.

I could not understand why Ira lied but I forgave her. I never even mentioned the conversation I had with the other ladies. Later, we decided to start an organization for teen girls in her apartment complex. I invited several girls I knew and she asked some girls from her complex. We were off to a great start. But a great start doesn't have a great finish if you have the wrong person working with you. After the organization was growing in attendance, she kicked me out like a pair of worn out shoes. She informed me that she was going to run it with another person.

I felt betrayed and hurt. I was crushed. This is the stuff that makes you get in your bed and not get up. Ira did not care that she had destroyed wonderful longtime friendships I had with others or that her lies caused me months of pain and betrayed my trust in her once again. When it came to picking her as a friend, or maybe she picked me, I really ended up on the short end of the stick.

I didn't hear from Ira for two years after that. One day, she just called me. She didn't call to say she was sorry or apologize for what she had done. She asked me to go into business with her again. Really? I couldn't believe she let those words come out of her mouth. I didn't go off on her. Maybe I should have, but I didn't. I just didn't respond. She got her answer in my silence. My response said it all. "Not today, not tomorrow, not ever!" I never heard back from her again.

Sometimes people do hurt your feelings; some on purpose and some that didn't even realize that they had. But as for me, I refuse to be friends with someone that is not in my corner. A relationship is a two-way street. Don't spend your time on people that never give toward the relationship or people you can't trust.

All the times I worked with Ira, I never even understood how she really felt about me. I didn't realize it, but she was jealous of me the whole time. I had no idea a person could be so destructive. One thing for sure, jealousy is a cruel stepsister and betrayal is a wicked stepmother. But as for this Cinderella, I had the other glass slipper. I slipped it on and kept right on steppin'.

CHAPTER NINE

DON'T BE LIMITED BY PAST MISTAKES

Life comes with decisions. That's just the way it is, girlfriend. Every once in awhile, my mind takes me on a road trip. If I don't stop it, I will be pulling up at the front door of *The House of Wrong Decisions* before I know it.

I don't dwell on the past often, but I can't believe some of the choices I made. I wondered how I got myself into some of the nasty, stinky, and messy situations. People I should have kept out of my life, jobs I should have turned down, or places I should have stayed away from. Many times I was on a merry-go-round of wrong decision craziness.

As I look back over many of the wrong decisions I have made, I refuse to get stuck back there. I realize that I can't do anything about the mistakes I made and neither can you. But what we can do is forgive ourselves and keep it moving. I don't know that person. She doesn't exist anymore and never will again.

One decision I regret making was buying my first car. I didn't know anything about how to check out a car's reliability. A couple selling the car brought it to my job and when I came out, they cranked the engine. The couple wasted no time telling me what a good deal I was getting. I believed them, so I paid them three hundred dollars cash and they left. I didn't even drive it before I purchased it. As I pulled out of the parking garage, I was so proud of myself because I was driving my first car!

I thought to myself, *I would not be riding the bus to work or college anymore.* Less than fifteen minutes later, that thing stopped on me. I got jipped, conned, and scammed! I can't tell you how many buses passed me up. There I was, stranded at night on a busy street in Montrose.

As my father pulled the car over to my Aunt Betty's house, where I was living at the time, I had plenty of time to think about the "Good deal I was getting." Then, he came the next day and put all kinds of parts on that green Ford Galaxy 500. So, I spent more money on parts. I didn't call the couple and share how wrong they were for selling me a lemon. Each time it stopped working, I called my dad to come over and fix it.

After I was married, my husband inherited the duties of mechanic. Each time that car broke down, he would fix it. We both could not wait until we had enough money to get rid of that car. Later, he found me a really nice dependable car. I didn't let that first bad car decision keep me from buying another car.

We may have experienced the result of wrong choices, but we should not let that determine if we quit. We have to be willing to get up, admit our mistakes, learn from them, and try again.

Don't allow your past mistakes keep you from trying again. Don't live in the world of "Would've, could've, should've." Mama once said, "Not everybody that invites you to come for a visit really means it." As for *The House of Wrong Decisions*, it didn't invite you so that means you are not welcomed there anymore.

CHAPTER TEN
GIRL, I STILL HAVE ISSUES

The things we will do to impress people so we can fit in. From what we wear to what we eat. From shaving our legs to plucking out perfectly good eyebrows or wearing high heels that are too tight but look good. I have been guilty of it all. I wanted to be accepted. Face it, we all do.

It was about fourth grade when I found out that even a gift gets you in the "You don't fit in our club" quicker than anything. Right before our Christmas break, my teacher asked the girls to bring a girl's gift and every boy to get a boy's gift for the Christmas Party. You know the one where you pick a number and find the present with that same number.

I knew what my mother had wrapped in the box I was holding in my hand for some poor unfortunate little girl. I remember worrying about what the other girls would think if they selected my gift.

On the teachers' desk were two glass fish bowls. One bowl was for the girls and the other was for the boys. She gave us two pieces of paper with the same number. One of them went on the gift and the other one went into the bowl. Before the party started, I put my gift under the stack of presents and hoped no one pulled my number.

Each girl reached into the bowl and pulled out a number. After that, we took turns unwrapping our gifts. No one was supposed to know who gave what gift, but after I unwrapped my present, Stella made it known to the whole class that I had gotten the gift she brought. In my eyes, Stella's family was wealthy, so as expected, I was not disappointed.

Then, Stella opened her gift, and as you probably guessed, she had pulled my number. "Socks! What kind of gift is that? Who would give socks as a gift?" She stared straight at me as she held up the box for all the other girls to see. Every single girl looked my way and started laughing.

Yes, a pair of pink socks with pink lace. I kept my head down as if I did not see them. Embarrassed? Very. That day, I just shut down. When I got home, I got in the bed and pulled the cover over my head. But the shame remained with me for years.

I should have been glad I had a gift at all. Mama was raising nine children and worked at a laundry during that time. She was struggling just to keep food on the table and a roof over our heads. She knew that a toy would only last for a week or two and soon be in the trash pile somewhere. Later that year, I remember Stella wore those same pink laced socks to school one day.

What's funny is I don't even remember Stella's gift. But I do remember how my Mama took her money and time. She didn't have to go to the store and buy those pink socks but out of the goodness in her heart, she did.

A lie will try to convince you that you are a misfit. It will keep you in a place where you feel unwanted. But the truth is that I don't know what I would have done if I had not forgiven all the "Stellas" I have met in life. Forgiveness is a choice and a process that I gladly embrace.

Don't stay in bed to cover up unforgiveness. When you have been hurt, don't stay there. Dealing with unforgiveness is like peeling an onion. If you let forgiveness cut away the hurt, it will keep peeling away layer after layer until you mean it. You may have to keep saying it, seventy times seven, that you forgive a person for what they did. Each time you do, you are peeling away every bit of ugly pain until it doesn't hurt anymore.

When it comes to forgiveness, my friend Debra Starr said it best when she would laugh and say, "Girl, I have issues, okay." Debra would tell me that she would pull off her shoes and wipe them off before entering her house. She would even put on gloves before she would touch the gas pump handle or push any buttons. Her actions were saying, *I have to protect me and I don't care what people think about it. I'm the only one at home and I can't afford to be sick behind someone's nasty habits or bad attitude about being clean.* She understood that there was nothing she could do about people, but she could keep herself safe.

Does it mean that you keep letting people hurt you over and over again? Of course you don't.

We must move on and refuse to stay under the cover with our heads covered up. We have to be determined enough to deal with situations that have made us want to hide. For all the girls like Stella that made us feel ashamed and rejected, we have to forgive them. Girl, we have issues, so that is why we have to choose to forgive them so we can protect our heart, body, mind, and soul. There will always be Stellas in the world, but one day they may need the very gift in us they made fun of.

CONCLUSION

After thinking about this book, I wanted to include stories that hopefully you can relate to and would encourage you not to give up on your dreams because of lies you heard.

So let me be one of those who inspire you to see past today and step into the amazing possibilities of tomorrow. If you want to get a degree, you are smart enough to do it. If that is your desire, go for it. If you want to write a book, you can do it. If you want take dance lessons, go for it.

I'm not saying you have to get a degree or even write a book. What I'm saying is that there is something wonderful and exciting past your bedroom door.

So I am taking this opportunity to hear you say, "I can do it!" I want you to know that those four words can inspire you if you let them. Write them on a piece of paper and pin it on your wall. Put it on your bathroom mirror and look at them throughout the day.

Will it be simple? No, not if you try to climb the mountain overnight. Can it happen? Of course it can, if you take one step at a time.

As I speak to you through these pages, you only have one life. Just one. The good part about life is that most of you will get opportunities to get up even when lies tell you otherwise. You have to keep getting up every morning and keep moving.

I believe in you. I want you to know that. I am looking forward to hearing what amazing things you are working towards and when you accomplish them. I am excited for you because I know you can.

CHAPTER ONE
STUDY NOTES

"Each Day is a New Opportunity to Unlock the Gifts and Talents Inside of You." - Deborah Elum

_____

_____

_____

_____

_____

_____

_____

_____

_____

_____

_____

CHAPTER TWO
STUDY NOTES

"Motivated People Always Light the Flame of Achievement in Others." - Deborah Elum

---

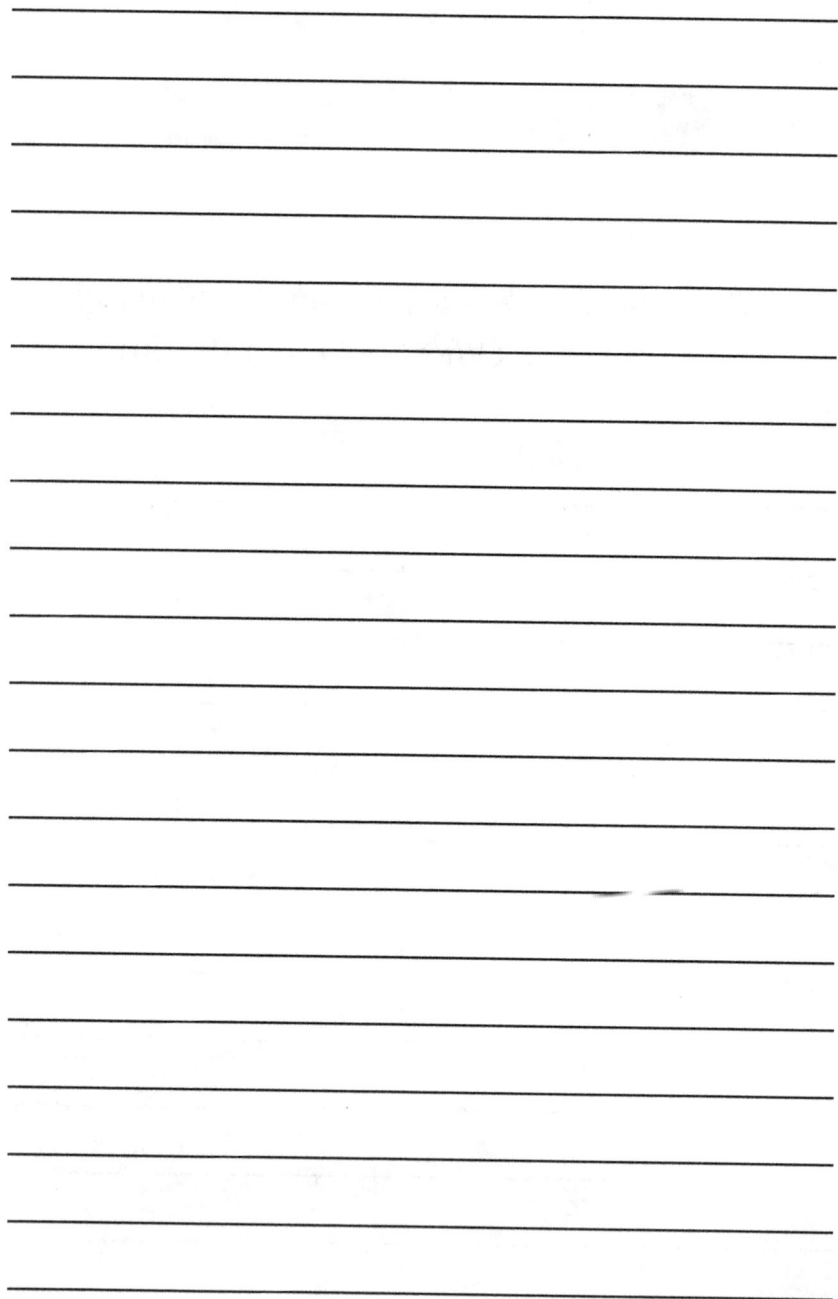

CHAPTER THREE
STUDY NOTES

"Just Because Someone Says 'No You Can't.'
Does Not Change Your 'Yes I Can.'" - Deborah Elum

_____

_____

_____

_____

_____

_____

_____

_____

_____

_____

_____

_____

CHAPTER FOUR
STUDY NOTES

"Goals Help Us Use Our Past to Step Into Our Future." - Deborah Elum

CHAPTER FIVE
STUDY NOTES

"Don't Let 'What If' Stop You from Doing the 'I Can.'" - Deborah Elum

_____

_____

_____

_____

_____

_____

_____

_____

_____

_____

_____

CHAPTER SIX
STUDY NOTES

"Your Destiny is Planted in the Soil of Your Heart. Keep the Weeds of Doubt Out." - Deborah Elum

_____

_____

_____

_____

_____

_____

_____

_____

_____

_____

_____

_____

_____

CHAPTER SEVEN
STUDY NOTES

"Success is Learning to Move Pass the Things That Do Not Matter." - Deborah Elum

_____

_____

_____

_____

_____

_____

_____

_____

_____

_____

_____

_____

_____

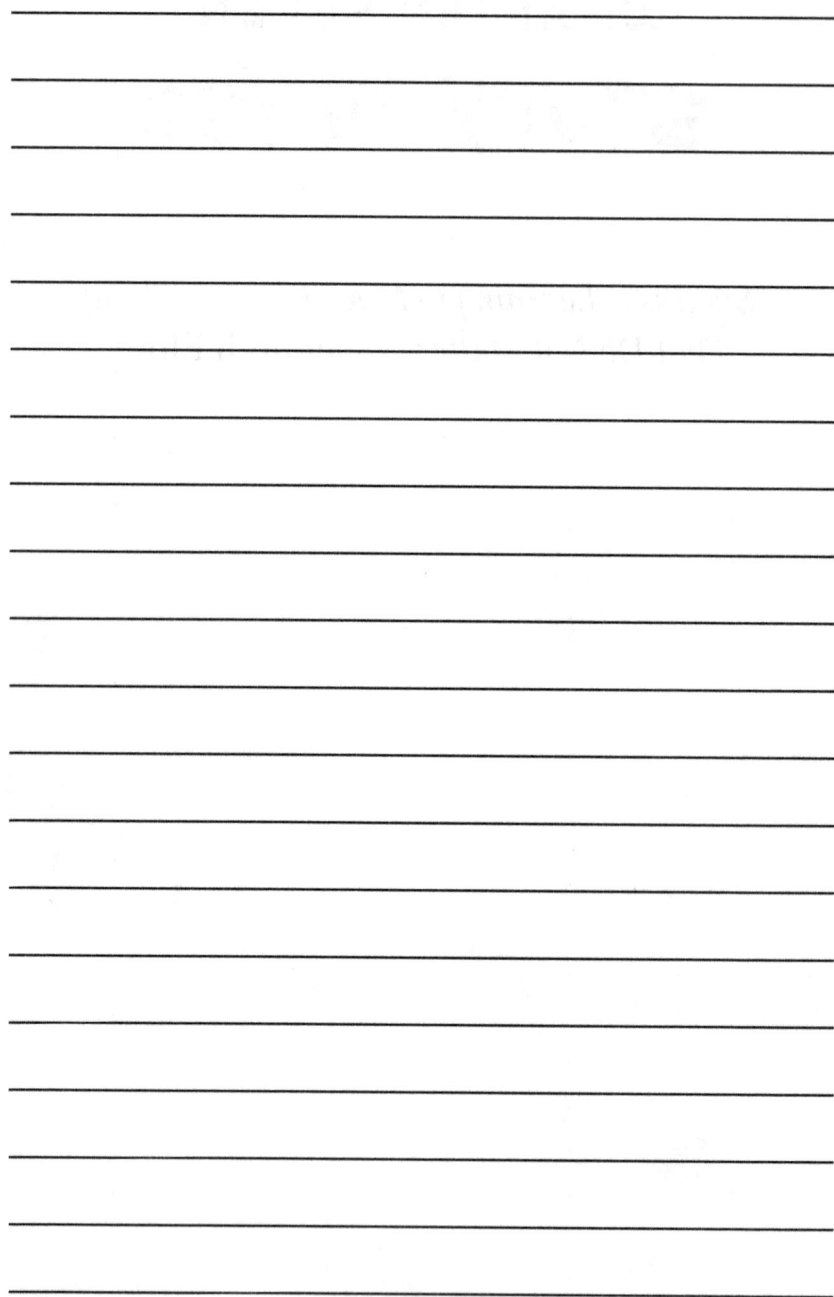

CHAPTER EIGHT
STUDY NOTES

"Make a Choice to Move Into Your Future."
- Deborah Elum

_____

_____

_____

_____

_____

_____

_____

_____

_____

_____

_____

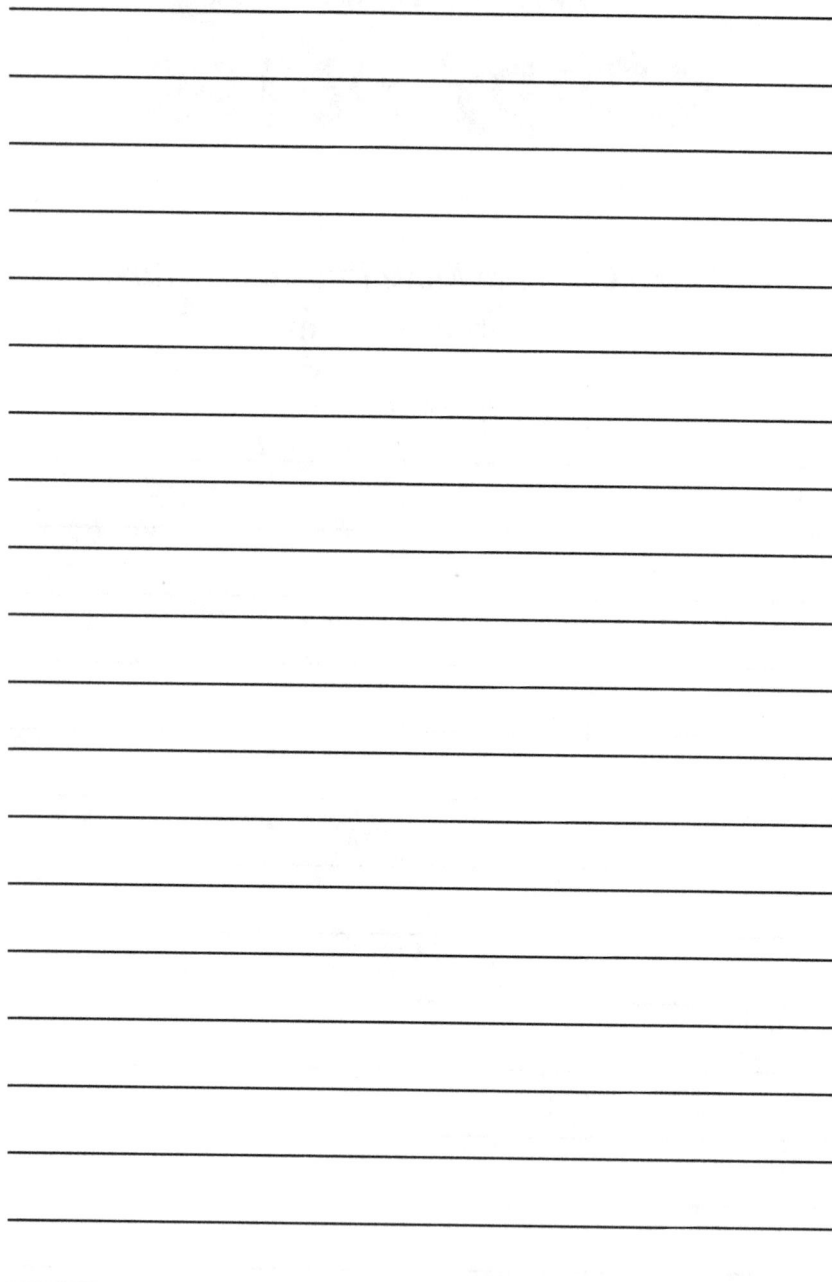

CHAPTER NINE
STUDY NOTES

"Every Day is an Opportunity to Dream of Possibilities and Start Working to Achieve Them."
- Deborah Elum

_____

_____

_____

_____

_____

_____

_____

_____

_____

_____

_____

_____

_____

CHAPTER TEN
STUDY NOTES

"Strength Comes When You Make a Decision to Do It." - Deborah Elum

_____

_____

_____

_____

_____

_____

_____

_____

_____

_____

_____

_____

_____

_____

www.ingramcontent.com/pod-product-compliance
Lightning Source LLC
Chambersburg PA
CBHW060135050426
42448CB00010B/2145